PERU 2016 HUMAN RIGHTS REPORT

EXECUTIVE SUMMARY

Peru is a constitutional, multiparty republic. Pedro Pablo Kuczynski, leader of the Peruanos Por el Kambio (Peruvians for Change) Party, won the June national elections in a vote widely considered free and fair.

Civilian authorities generally maintained effective control over the security forces.

The most serious human rights problems were violence against women, children, and lesbian, gay, bisexual, transgender, and intersex (LGBTI) persons; trafficking in persons; unlawful killings, and corruption and impunity that undermined the rule of law.

The following human rights problems also occurred: harsh prison conditions, lengthy pretrial detention, inordinate trial delays, intimidation of media, and threats towards human rights activists. In addition, there was discrimination against women, individuals with disabilities, members of racial and ethnic minority groups, indigenous persons, LGBTI persons, and persons with HIV/AIDS. Socio-environmental conflicts involving extractive industries and development projects occurred and sometimes turned violent. Other problems were weak labor law enforcement and the use of child labor, particularly in informal sectors. Corruption, human trafficking, and the labor and sexual exploitation of men, women, and children were common at illegal mining sites.

The government took steps to investigate, and in some cases prosecute or otherwise punish public officials accused of abuses. Officials sometimes engaged in corrupt practices with impunity.

The terrorist organization Sendero Luminoso (Shining Path) was responsible for killings and other abuses, including kidnapping and forced recruitment of child soldiers, extortion, and intimidation. The government maintained its active counterterrorism campaign against the Shining Path.

Section 1. Respect for the Integrity of the Person, Including Freedom from:

a. Arbitrary Deprivation of Life and other Unlawful or Politically Motivated Killings

After taking office on July 28, the Kuczynski administration launched an investigation into allegations that members of the Peruvian National Police (PNP) committed the extrajudicial killings of more than 20 criminal suspects from 2012 to 2015 as part of a scheme to receive awards and promotions. These allegations first surfaced in August. According to press and Ministry of Interior accounts, an "irregular" group of nine PNP officers and sub-officers allegedly paid informants to entrap individuals and provide regular police units with false intelligence, setting the stage for deadly confrontations. As of November, the government had produced no evidence that policy-level officials directed the alleged killings or had knowledge of the scheme.

On September 1, a special tribunal found 10 former army officers and enlisted persons guilty of killing 71 villagers, including 23 children, in the 1985 "Accomarca Massacre" that occurred during the conflict with the Shining Path terrorist group. The tribunal sentenced five officers to prison terms ranging from 23 to 25 years, including general Wilfredo Mori, lieutenant colonels Nelson Gonzalez Feria and Carlos Pastor Delgado Medina, and lieutenants Juan Rivera Rondon and Telmo Hurtado. Five low-ranking soldiers also received 10-year sentences. The tribunal acquitted six others, including general Jose Williams Zapata, for lack of sufficient evidence.

The Shining Path conducted several terrorist acts during the year that resulted in deaths and injuries (see section 1.g.), including an April 9 attack on army officers carrying electoral materials the day before the first round of national elections.

b. Disappearance

There were no reports of politically motivated disappearances during the year. The government, however, continued to address disappearances that occurred during the internal conflict of 1980-2000. The Truth and Reconciliation Commission estimated that more than 15,000 persons disappeared during this period.

The government approved a new law in July that requires the Ministry of Justice to oversee the recovery, identification, and return of the approximately 15,000 "disappeared" human remains from the internal conflict as a humanitarian priority. The law requires the government to simultaneously collect evidence and proceed with criminal investigations.

On September 27, a court found Vladimiro Montesinos, the intelligence chief and chief advisor to former president Alberto Fujimori, guilty of the disappearance and murder of two students and one professor in 1993. Both Fujimori and Montesinos were already serving 25-year prison sentences for human rights abuses. By law the decision did not add additional time to Montesinos' prison sentence.

c. Torture and Other Cruel, Inhuman, or Degrading Treatment or Punishment

The law prohibits such practices. Local nongovernmental organizations (NGOs), however, reported that torture remained a problem, primarily within the police force and stated the government did not effectively prevent and punish those who committed such abuses.

According to the local NGO Human Rights Commission, many victims did not file formal complaints about their alleged torture, and those who did so purportedly had difficulty obtaining judicial redress and adequate compensation.

Prison and Detention Center Conditions

Prison conditions remained harsh for most of the country's inmates, due to overcrowding, poor sanitation, inadequate nutrition and health care, and corruption among guards, which included guards smuggling weapons and drugs into the prisons. Guards received little to no training or supervision.

Physical Conditions: As of June the National Penitentiary Institute (INPE) reported that the national penitentiary system had 77,086 prisoners in 67 facilities originally designed for 32,890 prisoners. On July 10, the government opened a new prison in Cochamarca, which was built to hold 1,300 prisoners. As of January, the San Juan de Lurigancho men's prison held 9,958 prisoners in a facility designed for 3,204. The Sarita Colonia prison in the Callao Region had a designed capacity of 572 persons but held 3,296 in January. Prisons for women also were overcrowded. The Santa Monica women's prison in Chorrillos was designed for 450 inmates but held 823.

INPE operated 31 of the 68 active prisons, the PNP had jurisdiction over five, the PNP and INPE operated 31 prisons jointly, and INPE and the army jointly operated one prison. The judicial system used pretrial detention centers located at police stations, judiciary buildings, and the Palace of Justice to hold pretrial detainees temporarily.

Prison guards and fellow inmates reportedly abused prisoners, and inmates killed fellow inmates during the year. Inmates had intermittent access to potable water, bathing facilities were inadequate, kitchen facilities were unhygienic, and prisoners often slept in hallways and common areas for lack of cell space. Prisoners with money had access to cell phones, illegal drugs, and meals prepared outside the prison; prisoners who lacked funds experienced much more difficult conditions.

Most prisons provided access to basic medical care, but there was a shortage of doctors, and inmates complained of having to pay for medical attention. Tuberculosis and HIV/AIDS reportedly remained at near-epidemic levels. The Ombudsman's Office continued to report the incidence of tuberculosis, and HIV/AIDS infections were significantly higher in prisons than in the general population. The Ombudsman's Office also reported insufficient accessibility and inadequate facilities for prisoners with disabilities. Prisons lacked specialized medical equipment needed for prisoners with disabilities, such as wheelchairs and transferrable beds. Low accessibility to adequate psychological care for prisoners with mental disabilities was also reported.

Administration: Independent and government authorities investigated allegations of mistreatment in prisons and made the results of their investigations public.

Independent Monitoring: The government permitted monitoring visits by independent human rights and international humanitarian law observers. Between January and October, International Committee of the Red Cross officials made 12 unannounced visits to inmates in 12 different prisons and detention centers and individually monitored approximately 95 individual prisoners. During the year, the Ombudsman's Office representatives made 150 visits to Lima and provincial prisons and 30 visits to juvenile detention centers.

d. Arbitrary Arrest or Detention

The constitution and law prohibit arbitrary arrest and detention, and the government generally observed these prohibitions. The government constitutionally suspended the right to freedom from arrest without warrant in designated emergency zones (see section 1.g.).

Role of the Police and Security Apparatus

The PNP, with a force of approximately 114,830 personnel, is responsible for all areas of law enforcement and internal security, including migration and border security. The PNP functioned under the authority of the Ministry of Interior. The armed forces, with approximately 100,000 personnel, are responsible for external security under the authority of the Ministry of Defense but also have limited domestic security responsibilities, particularly in the Valley of the Apurimac, Ene, and Mantaro Rivers (VRAEM) emergency zone.

Corruption and a high rate of acquittals in civilian courts for military personnel accused of crimes remained serious problems. The Public Ministry conducted investigations, although access to evidence held by the Ministry of Defense was not always forthcoming. The Ombudsman's Office can also investigate cases and submit conclusions to the Public Ministry for follow-up. The Ministries of Interior and Defense employed internal mechanisms to investigate allegations of security force abuse. The Ministry of Interior's Office of Inspector General reported that it disciplined approximately 7,400 police officers from January to August.

The Public Ministry is charged with witness protection responsibilities but lacked resources to provide sufficient training to prosecutors and police officers, conceal identities, or furnish logistical support to witnesses.

Police continued operating under a use of force doctrine adopted in 2015. When a police action causes death or injury, the law requires an administrative investigation and notification to the appropriate oversight authorities. The law is applicable to all police force members and defines the principles, rules, situations, and limitations for police use of force and firearms.

Arrest Procedures and Treatment of Detainees

The law permits police to detain persons for investigations. The law requires a written judicial warrant based on sufficient evidence for an arrest, unless authorities apprehend the alleged perpetrator of a crime in the act. Only judges may authorize detentions. Authorities are required to arraign arrested persons within 24 hours, except in cases of terrorism, drug trafficking, or espionage, for which arraignment must take place within 15 days. In remote areas, arraignment must take place as soon as practicably possible. Military authorities must turn over persons they detain to police within 24 hours. The law requires police to file a report with the Public Ministry within 24 hours after an arrest. The Public Ministry, in turn, must issue its own assessment of the legality of the police action in the arrest, and authorities respected this requirement.

Judges have 24 hours to decide whether to release a suspect or continue detention, and the judiciary respected this provision. A functioning bail system exists, but many poor defendants lack the means to post bail. By law detainees are allowed access to family members and a lawyer of their choice. Police may detain suspected terrorists incommunicado for 10 days.

Pretrial Detention: Lengthy pretrial detention continued to be a problem. In January authorities had sentenced only 38,198 of the 77,298 detainees held in detention facilities and prisons. Delays were due mainly to judicial inefficiency, corruption, and staff shortages. Under the criminal procedure code, the law requires the release of prisoners held more than nine months whom the justice system has not tried and sentenced; the period is 18 months for complex cases. In one prominent case, a judge released regional Governor Gregorio Santos, who was accused of corruption, from prison on July 27 after 23 months of pretrial imprisonment. During this time Santos was allowed to participate as a candidate in regional (2014) and national (2016) elections.

Detainee's Ability to Challenge Lawfulness of Detention before a Court: Persons arrested or detained, regardless of whether on criminal or other grounds, are entitled to challenge in court the legal basis or arbitrary nature of their detention and obtain prompt release and compensation if found to have been unlawfully detained.

e. Denial of Fair Public Trial

The constitution provides for an independent judiciary. NGOs and other advocates alleged the judiciary often did not operate independently, was not consistently impartial, and was subject to political influence and corruption. Authorities generally respected court orders from the judiciary.

Trial Procedures

The law provides for the right to a fair and public trial, and the judiciary generally enforced this right, although reports of corruption in the judicial system were common. The government continued the implementation, begun in 2006, of a criminal procedure code designed to streamline the penal process. As of October, the government had introduced the code in 28 of the 31 judicial districts, although implementation in the largest judicial districts--Lima and Callao--remained pending. The code requires public hearings for each case and assigns investigative responsibility to public prosecutors and police.

The law presumes all defendants innocent. The government also must promptly inform defendants in detail of the charges against them and provide defendants a fair and public trail without undue delay. Defendants also have the right to communicate with an attorney of their choice or have one provided at public expense; however, state-provided attorneys often have poor training. Although the law grants citizens the right to trial in their own language, language services for non-Spanish speakers were sometimes unavailable. This deficiency primarily affected indigenous people living in the highlands and Amazon Regions. In a case from 2015, however, a court in Puno issued its decision in the Aymara indigenous language, which is prevalent in the region. As of October, the decision was on appeal to a court in Lima, and any additional court findings would use Aymara. The law also gives all defendants the right to adequate time and facilities to prepare for their defense.

Defendants generally had access to government-held evidence related to their cases. Exceptions reportedly occurred in some human rights abuse cases from the 1980-2000 period. In many of these cases, the government classified related documents as secret and subject to disclosure limitations under the law. Defendants have the right to confront adverse witnesses and present their own witnesses and evidence. The government cannot compel defendants to testify or confess to a crime. Defendants may appeal verdicts to a superior court and ultimately to the Supreme Court. The Constitutional Tribunal may rule on cases involving issues such as habeas corpus or the constitutionality of laws.

Political Prisoners and Detainees

There were no reports of political prisoners or detainees during the year.

Civil Judicial Procedures and Remedies

Citizens may seek civil remedies for human rights violations, but court cases often take years to resolve. Press reports, NGOs, and other sources continued to allege that persons outside the judiciary frequently corrupted or influenced judges.

f. Arbitrary or Unlawful Interference with Privacy, Family, Home, or Correspondence

The law prohibits such actions, and the government generally respected these prohibitions. The government's declaration of emergency zones in the VRAEM and Callao Region, due to drug trafficking and criminal activity, suspended the right to home inviolability.

g. Abuses in Internal Conflict

The Shining Path terrorist organization was responsible for killings and other human rights abuses during the year.

Killings: The Shining Path terrorist organization conducted several terrorist attacks against military personnel in the VRAEM emergency zone. On April 9, the day before the first round of the national elections, Shining Path members ambushed and killed eight soldiers and two civilians.

The Public Ministry continued to investigate the killing of a pregnant woman that occurred during a 2014 counterterrorist operation in Uchuy Sihuis, Huancavelica Region.

Abductions: The government, NGOs, and journalists reported the Shining Path abducted persons, including children, to work for the terrorist organization.

Physical Abuse, Punishment, and Torture: The government, NGOs, and journalists reported the Shining Path continued to use forced labor.

Child Soldiers: The government, NGOs, and journalists reported the Shining Path recruited and used child soldiers under forced labor conditions, and in combat and drug-trafficking activities, including crop production and chemical laboratories. The Shining Path kidnapped or recruited children from nearby towns, while others apparently were the children of Shining Path members.

See also the Department of State's *Trafficking in Persons Report* at www.state.gov/j/tip/rls/tiprpt/.

Section 2. Respect for Civil Liberties, Including:

a. Freedom of Speech and Press

The constitution provides for freedom of speech and press, and the government mainly respected these rights during the year. Generally, an independent press and a functioning democratic political system promoted freedom of speech and press.

<u>Violence and Harassment</u>: Numerous journalists alleged police, protesters, and company personnel assaulted and threatened them while covering various protests and incidents of social unrest. The Press and Society Institute (IPYS) reported that the most common type of threats was against local radio and television broadcast journalists who were investigating local government authorities for corruption. IPYS alleged the aggressors were often local and regional government officials, such as mayors and regional governors.

On November 21, alleged paid assassins killed radio journalist Hernan Choquepata Ordonez as he arrived at work in the coastal province of Camana, Arequipa Region. Reports suggest Choquepata was killed after he criticized mayors of the municipalities of Camana and Mariscal Caceres. A police investigation continued at year's end.

As of September investigations were pending into the 2014 deaths of investigative journalist Fernando Raymondi, whom an unknown gunman killed, and journalist Donny Buchelli Cueva, who was reportedly tortured and killed in his home, allegedly for criticizing mayoral candidates' professional credentials and behavior.

As of November the National Journalists Association reported 115 cases of aggression and harassment, compared with 64 as of September 2015, and IPYS issued 18 alerts, compared with 21 in 2015.

<u>Censorship or Content Restrictions</u>: Some media, most notably in the provinces outside of Lima, continued to practice self-censorship due to fear of local government reprisal.

<u>Libel/Slander Laws</u>: The law criminalizes libel, and officials reportedly used libel charges to intimidate reporters. A court found *Caretas* journalist Rafo Leon guilty of defamation in May for criticizing former *El Comercio* newspaper editor Martha Meier. The judge sentenced Leon to a suspended one-year sentence, contingent on his "good behavior," and fined him 6,000 soles ($1,800). Journalists, NGOs, press freedom activists, the Ombudsman's Office, and politicians across the political spectrum condemned the court's ruling. The Supreme Court overturned the decision on September 8, ruling Leon's criticism qualified as legitimate opinion that did not amount to defamation.

<u>National Security</u>: The law defines all national security and defense information as secret. In June Defense Minister Jakke Valakivi announced an investigation of journalists working for the news program *Panorama* for allegedly breaching

national security when they presented classified documents on television as evidence of military corruption. Journalists, NGOs, and a broad array of politicians, including then president-elect Kuczynski, condemned the investigation, noting the act revealed information in the public interest. The Kuczynski government, which supported the journalists, declared it would decline to investigate, and the case had not advanced as of October.

Nongovernmental Impact: Some media reported that narcotics traffickers and illegal mining operations threatened press freedom by intimidating journalists who reported information that undermined their operations.

Internet Freedom

The government did not restrict or disrupt access to the internet or censor online content, and there were no credible reports that the government monitored private online communications without appropriate legal authority.

According to the National Statistics and Information Institute, 62 percent of the population used the internet. A September report from the Ipsos Peru polling firm found 39 percent of citizens accessed the internet at home, and 21 percent accessed it exclusively via a mobile device.

Academic Freedom and Cultural Events

There were no government restrictions on academic freedom or cultural events.

b. Freedom of Peaceful Assembly and Association

The constitution provides for the freedom of assembly and association.

Freedom of Assembly

The law does not require a permit for public demonstrations, but organizers must report the type of demonstration planned and coordinate its intended location to the appropriate regional representative. The government suspended freedom of assembly in certain emergency zones where armed elements of the Shining Path and drug traffickers operated as well as in regions suffering from crime and public health crises.

The government may restrict or prohibit demonstrations in specific times and places for public safety or health. Police used tear gas and occasional force to disperse protesters in various demonstrations. Although most were peaceful, protests in some areas turned violent, resulting in deaths and injuries (see section 6, Other Societal Violence and Discrimination).

On October 14, the police shot and killed one individual during a clash over noise and pollution allegedly caused by Las Bambas mining trucks using a secondary road in the Apurimac Region.

Freedom of Association

The law provides for freedom of association; however, there were reports the government did not sufficiently respect this right, particularly with regard to minority religious groups' right to government registration and equal access to some benefits. In July the government adopted new regulations pertaining to the 2010 Religious Freedom Law that eliminated the requirement for official registration, which resolved this concern.

c. Freedom of Religion

See the Department of State's *International Religious Freedom Report* at www.state.gov/religiousfreedomreport/.

d. Freedom of Movement, Internally Displaced Persons, Protection of Refugees, and Stateless Persons

The law provides for freedom of internal movement, foreign travel, emigration, and repatriation, and the government generally respected these rights. The government cooperated with the Office of the UN High Commissioner for Refugees (UNHCR) and other humanitarian organizations to provide protection and assistance to internally displaced persons, refugees, returning refugees, asylum seekers, stateless persons, or other persons of concern.

The government and civil society organizations estimated there were 120,000 foreign citizens legally residing in the country, and between 20,000 and 100,000 foreigners residing under irregular circumstances.

In-country Movement: The government maintained two emergency zones in parts of six regions, where it restricted freedom of movement in an effort to maintain public peace and restore internal order. In 2015 the government declared an emergency zone in Callao due to increased crime stemming from gang and drug-trafficking violence.

Narcotics traffickers and Shining Path members at times interrupted the free movement of persons by establishing roadblocks in sections of the VRAEM emergency zone. Individuals protesting against extractive industry projects also occasionally established roadblocks throughout the country.

Internally Displaced Persons

The situation of former internally displaced persons (IDPs) remained difficult to assess. According to UNHCR, the number of IDPs remained unknown, since officials registered relatively few.

The governmental Reparations Council continued to assist victims of the 1980-2000 internal conflict with the Shining Path and the Tupac Amaru Revolutionary Movement terrorist groups. The Quechua and other Andean indigenous populations were disproportionately represented among IDPs, since the conflict took place primarily within the Andean Region. The council continued to compile a registry of victims and identify communities eligible for reparations. Some victims and family members lacking proper identity documents experienced difficulties registering for reparations.

Protection of Refugees

Access to Asylum: The law provides for the granting of asylum or refugee status, and the government has established a system for providing protection to refugees. The government cooperated with UNHCR and recognized the Catholic Migration Commission as the official provider of technical assistance to refugees. The commission also advised citizens who feared persecution and sought asylum abroad. The government provided protection to refugees on a renewable, year-to-year basis, in accordance with commission recommendations. The asylum requests grew sharply during the year, from approximately 400 cases in 2015 to approximately 1,600 between January and August. Approximately 60 percent of the 2016 asylum requests came from Venezuelan citizens, who generally did not qualify as refugees. There were 32 Syrian refugees as of September; the government has granted refugee status to every Syrian who has requested it.

<u>Durable Solutions</u>: There was no resettlement program, but the government received persons recognized as refugees in other nations and provided some administrative support toward their integration. UNHCR provided such refugees humanitarian and emergency aid, legal assistance, documentation, and, in exceptional cases, voluntary return and family reunification.

<u>Temporary Protection</u>: As of September the government provided temporary protection to more than 1,000 individuals awaiting a decision state on their refugee status.

Section 3. Freedom to Participate in the Political Process

The law provides citizens the ability to choose their government in free and fair periodic elections held by secret ballot and based on universal and equal suffrage.

Elections and Political Participation

<u>Recent Elections</u>: On July 28, Pedro Pablo Kuczynski assumed the presidency after a second round of presidential elections. He won by 0.2 percent (approximately 40,000 votes), the closest margin of victory in the country's history. Kuczynski's second-round opponent, Keiko Fujimori, conceded the election. Domestic and international observers declared the nationwide elections-- held in April (for president, the National Congress, and the Andean Parliament) and in June (a second round for the presidential race only) to be fair and transparent, despite controversy over the exclusion of two candidates for administrative violations of election-related laws.

The national electoral authority's disqualification of leading presidential candidates in the months prior to national elections led to increased calls for electoral reform by both national and international institutions.

<u>Political Parties and Political Participation</u>: Political parties operated without restriction or outside interference, although many remained weak institutions dominated by individual personalities. By law groups that advocate the violent overthrow of the government and express ideologies incompatible with democracy cannot register as political parties.

<u>Participation of Women and Minorities</u>: No laws limit participation of women and minorities in the political process, and they participated. As of December there were 36 women in Congress, five women were cabinet members, and one of the

two vice presidents was a woman. Self-identified minorities in Congress included two Afro-Peruvians and one indigenous member. Two members of Congress self-identified as gay.

Section 4. Corruption and Lack of Transparency in Government

The law provides criminal penalties for officials engaged in corruption; however, the government did not always implement the law effectively, and officials often engaged in corrupt practices with impunity. There were numerous reports of government corruption during the year. Citizens continued to view corruption as a pervasive problem in all branches of national, regional, and local governments.

Corruption: The governmental Public Service Office, which reports directly to the cabinet, manages a registry of former government officials who are no longer eligible for public service due to corruption crimes. Between 2014 and November 2016, various courts had convicted three of 26 former and sitting regional governors of corruption charges, and another six remained under preliminary or full investigation.

There were allegations of widespread corruption in the judicial system during the year. Although not fully implemented in Lima and Callao, the government applied the new criminal procedure code to corruption cases in these judicial districts. In 2015 authorities dismissed then attorney general Carlos Ramos Heredia for impeding investigations into corruption networks orchestrated by former regional governor Cesar Alvarez and businessman Rodolfo Orellana. In 2014 authorities had arrested Alvarez for homicide and corruption-related crimes and Orellana for fraud and money laundering. Both were accused of bribing vast networks of police officers, judges, prosecutors, and other public officials to protect themselves from prosecution. A special congressional investigative commission, the Public Ministry, and the National Magistrates Council continued investigations into the networks. As of November the government renewed its pretrial detention of Alvarez, and the case against him and Orellana remained pending.

Members of Congress enjoy congressional immunity and may not be prosecuted for any acts during their time in the legislature. In the case of flagrant crimes, the judicial branch may request that Congress lift immunity and allow the arrest of a member. By law congressional immunity does not apply to crimes committed before the member was sworn in, but it impeded most prosecutions in practice.

Corruption in prisons remained a serious problem during the year, with continuing cases of guards cooperating with criminal bosses who oversaw the smuggling of guns and drugs into prisons. There were several reports of military corruption, impunity, and resistance in providing evidence on military personnel under investigation for human rights abuses committed during the country's internal conflict against the Shining Path. Security forces continued to strengthen accountability with mandatory human rights training.

Financial Disclosure: By law most public officials must submit personal financial information to the Office of the Comptroller General prior to taking office and periodically thereafter. The Comptroller General's Office monitors and verifies disclosures, but the law was not strongly enforced. Administrative sanctions for noncompliance range from 30-day to one-year suspensions, include bans on signing government contracts, and culminate with a ban from holding government office. The comptroller makes disclosures available to the public. On November 26, the government issued anew law under congressionally granted legislative powers to enable the Superintendency of Banks' Financial Intelligence Unit to access individual or corporate tax records and bank accounts to investigate allegations of money laundering and other crimes.

Public Access to Information: The law provides for public access to government information, and most ministries and central offices provided some information on websites. Implementation of the law was incomplete, particularly outside of Lima, where few citizens exercised or understood their right to information. The ombudsman encouraged regional governments to adopt more-transparent practices for releasing information and monitored their compliance with the requirement for public hearings at least twice a year.

The law has a narrow list of exceptions and grounds for not releasing certain government records. Government officials may exclude the release of classified information, information concerning national security, intelligence, police investigations, and details surrounding advanced technology. The law requires a reasonable timeline for officials to disclose financial information. The Ombudsman's Office reported that response times to information requests submitted to the Constitutional Court were often lengthy, varying from 18 to 36 months. The law also imposes administrative, but not criminal sanctions for noncompliance.

Section 5. Governmental Attitude Regarding International and Nongovernmental Investigation of Alleged Violations of Human Rights

A variety of domestic and international human rights groups generally operated without government restriction, investigating and publishing their findings on human rights cases. Government officials were somewhat cooperative and responsive to their views.

Human rights activists continued to express concern about their safety while working in areas with social unrest, including in the regions of Cajamarca, Cusco, Madre de Dios, and Arequipa, where social conflicts existed, particularly over natural resource extractive activities. They also alleged locally elected government authorities harassed activists, especially in areas where officials faced corruption charges and links to criminal activities. The activists claimed that the slow, ineffective process for sanctioning harassers essentially supported impunity.

In an October 2016 report, the Ombudsman's Office listed 154 active social conflicts. More than 70 percent of these conflicts were socio-environmental related and involved community based protests against large-scale mining projects. As a result, protesters were often wounded and occasionally killed by security forces. Similarly, indigenous leaders and environmental activists working on socio-environmental disputes have been killed and harassed, such as the unsolved 2014 case of four killed Ashaninka indigenous leaders (see section 6).

Government Human Rights Bodies: The Ministry of Justice and Human Rights, and in particular the Vice Ministry of Human Rights and Access to Justice, oversees human rights issues at the national level. The Ministry of Interior and the Ministry of Women and Vulnerable Populations also have significant human rights roles.

The independent Office of the Ombudsman operated without government or party interference, and NGOs, civil society organizations, and the public considered it effective. An acting ombudsman led the institution until August 6, when Congress elected a permanent ombudsman to the position.

Congressional committees included Justice and Human Rights; Women and the Family; Labor; Andean, Amazonian, Afro-Peruvian Peoples and Environment and Ecology; Health, Population, and Persons with Disabilities; and Women and Social Development.

Section 6. Discrimination, Societal Abuses, and Trafficking in Persons

Women

<u>Rape and Domestic Violence</u>: The law criminalizes rape, including spousal rape, with penalties of six to eight years in prison. Femicide is a crime and carries a minimum sentence of 15 years' imprisonment for those convicted of killing a woman if she is an immediate relative, spouse, or partner. The law establishes sentences of up to life in prison when the victim is a minor, pregnant, or has a disability. Enforcement of these laws, however, was often ineffective.

The law prohibits domestic violence, and penalties range from one month to six years in prison. The law also authorizes judges and prosecutors to prevent the convicted spouse or parent from returning to the family home and authorizes the victim's relatives and unrelated persons living in the home to file complaints of domestic violence. It also allows health professionals to document injuries. The law requires a police investigation of domestic violence to take place within five days of a complaint and obliges authorities to extend protection to female victims of domestic violence. Enforcement of these laws, however, was lax.

Civil society experts claimed that persons significantly underreported rape and domestic violence complaints, due to stigma, mistreatment, weak confidence in the authorities, and a fear of retribution, including further violence. Studies showed that only 27 percent of women age 18 or more who suffered an attack reported it, and most reports did not result in proper sanctions.

Violence against women and girls--including rape, spousal abuse, and sexual, physical, and psychological abuse--remained serious national problems. As of September the Ministry of Women and Vulnerable Populations documented 38,567 cases of violence against women, an 18 percent increase from 2015. Through September the Ministry of Women also reported 85 femicides, compared with 64 in 2015 (a 33 percent increase), and 171 femicide attempts, compared with 124 in 2015 (a 38 percent increase). The Women's Ministry also reported that 70 percent of women had suffered at least one incident of serious physical or psychological abuse. Additionally, the ombudsman found that 40 percent of police stations did not have adequate facilities to interview victims and the majority of police officers and prosecution office personnel did not have specialized training in the treatment of abused women. In one particularly emblematic case, in September a 15-year-old girl in the city of Ayacucho died two days after four assailants, two of whom were minors, raped her. The police captured all four assailants who were in detention awaiting trial.

The Ministry of Women and Vulnerable Populations operated the Women's Emergency Program. The program consisted of 238 service centers with police, prosecutors, counselors, and public welfare agents to help victims of domestic abuse. The program also addressed the legal, psychological, social, and medical problems of victims. NGOs expressed concerns about the program's quality and quantity, particularly in rural areas. In addition, the ministry operated a toll-free hotline and implemented projects to sensitize government employees and the citizenry to domestic violence.

The government continued through its national program against family and sexual violence to provide technical assistance to regional governments to support temporary shelters in nine of 25 regions. NGOs and members of Congress stated there were not enough shelters for victims of domestic violence and trafficking in persons.

On August 13, thousands of persons, representing a broad cross section of the population, joined the "Ni Una Menos" (Not One Woman Less) peaceful, nation-wide march to protest violence against women. Between 50,000 and 200,000 persons marched in Lima, including domestic violence survivors, civil society organizations, celebrities, President Kuczynski, ministers, and members of Congress.

On August 9, the judiciary created a Gender Justice Commission composed of women judges responsible for promoting a gender justice perspective within the judiciary. The judiciary also created 24 jurisdictional bodies to address exclusively domestic violence cases.

Sexual Harassment: Sexual harassment was a serious problem. In 2015 Congress approved a law that criminalizes sexual harassment in public spaces. Under this law sexual harassment is defined as unsolicited comments, actions, and touching of a sexual nature that is unwanted by the female or male victim. Sexual harassment in the workplace, however, is not a criminal offense. Instead, workplace harassment is a labor rights violation subject to administrative punishment. The law defines sexual harassment poorly, according to NGOs, and government enforcement was minimally effective. There were no available statistics on sexual harassers prosecuted, convicted, or punished.

Reproductive Rights: Couples and individuals have the right to decide the number, spacing, and timing of their children; manage their reproductive health; and have access to the information and means to do so, free from discrimination, coercion, or violence.

In August the Constitutional Court reversed the 2009 ban on emergency oral contraception in public-health policies, ordering the Ministry of Health to include the "morning after pill" in its reproductive health and family planning policies. The government accepted the decision and restarted the distribution of the pills in its health-care system in September.

In July the government issued a ruling that cleared jailed former president Alberto Fujimori and his health ministers of criminal responsibility for forced sterilizations in the late 1990s as part of a nationwide family planning program. The public prosecutor ruled that individual medical personnel were responsible for the isolated cases where women were sterilized without consent and recommended that five doctors be charged. Women's rights activists protested against the ruling, which stated that the reproductive health and family planning program had not violated human rights as part of a state policy.

Discrimination: The law provides for equality between men and women and prohibits discrimination against women with regard to marriage, divorce, and property rights. While the law prohibits discrimination in employment and educational opportunities based on gender, there was a persistent underrepresentation of women in high-ranking positions, and the arbitrary dismissal of pregnant women and workplace discrimination remained common. The law stipulates that women should receive equal pay for equal work, but women often were paid less than men. The National Statistics Bureau estimated that as of September, women received on average 81 percent the average income of men.

Children

Birth Registration: Citizenship is derived either by birth within the country's territory or from one's parents. Problems with government registration of births continued, although the government made significant efforts and progress. After a child is born and registered, parents receive their child's national identification card, which is periodically renewed.

Obtaining a national identity document requires a birth certificate, which was a problem in the most remote rural areas, where many births occurred at home and were not registered. As a result, poor indigenous women and children who inhabit these remote areas disproportionately lacked identity documents. Undocumented citizens faced social and political barriers to accessing government services, including running for public office or holding title to land. Government representatives and NGOs assessed that undocumented citizens were particularly vulnerable to labor exploitation, human trafficking, and crime. To address this problem, in 2015 the government launched the Itinerant Social Action Platforms, which continued to send navy boats to rivers in the Amazon Region to distribute basic health-care and registry services to remote indigenous communities.

Education: The constitution stipulates that primary and secondary education is compulsory, universal, and free through the secondary level. Nevertheless, citizens and NGOs continued to claim that education was not completely free, and fees for parental associations, administration, and educational materials greatly reduced access for lower-income families.

Child Abuse: Children continued to suffer from violence and sexual abuse, which remained serious problems. Many cases went unreported because societal norms regarded such abuse as a family problem to be resolved privately.

The government continued to support overnight shelters for abandoned or neglected children and child victims of violence, including child trafficking victims, in 14 of 25 regions. The Women's Emergency Program received information through child rights and welfare protection offices and assisted child victims of violence. The Children's Bureau coordinated government policies and programs for children and adolescents. At the grassroots level, child rights and welfare protection offices resolved complaints ranging from child physical and sexual abuse to abandonment and failure to pay child support. Provincial or district governments operated approximately half of these offices, while schools, churches, and NGOs ran the others. Law students staffed most of the units, particularly in rural districts. When these offices could not resolve disputes, officials usually referred cases to the Public Ministry's local prosecutor offices, whose adjudications were legally binding and had the same force as court judgments.

Early and Forced Marriage: The legal minimum age of marriage is 18. The law allows minors older than 16 to marry with civil judge authorization.

Sexual Exploitation of Children: The law prohibits exploiting children in prostitution and penalizes perpetrators with five to 12 years in prison. During the year government officials, police, NGOs, civil society leaders, and journalists identified numerous cases of child prostitution. The country remained a destination for child sex tourism, with Lima, Cusco, Loreto, and Madre de Dios as the principal locations. Involvement in child sex tourism is punishable by four to 10 years in prison. The Foreign Trade and Tourism Ministry disseminated information about the problem in coordination with NGOs and local governments as part of a campaign to combat child exploitation.

The minimum age for consensual sex is 14. Statutory rape law stipulates different penalties for different rape offenses. A conviction of rape of a minor younger than age 14 would lead to penalties ranging from 25 years to life in prison. The law prohibits child pornography, and the penalty for conviction of involvement in child pornography is four to 12 years' imprisonment and a fine. The law also prohibits adults from using deceit, abuse of power, or the vulnerability of a teenager to have sex with a minor under age 18.

In September 2016 the Permanent Chamber of the Supreme Court absolved a bar owner who had employed a 14-year-old girl found engaged in commercial sexual exploitation. The Supreme Court's decision, accepting the owner's argument that the girl's job was only to encourage men to drink and that the owner was unaware she was having sex with patrons, was heavily criticized. Following widespread condemnation, the National Judiciary Council launched an investigation into the decision and the Permanent Chamber's five-judge panel.

Child Soldiers: The government, NGOs, and journalists reported the Shining Path used child soldiers (see section 1.g.). The Ombudsman's Office reported the army had no cases of enlisting underage soldiers during the year.

International Child Abductions: The country is a party to the 1980 Hague Convention on the Civil Aspects of International Child Abduction. See the Department of State's *Annual Report on International Parental Child Abduction* at travel.state.gov/content/childabduction/en/legal/compliance.html.

Anti-Semitism

Estimates of the Jewish population ranged from 3,000-4,000 persons. There were no reports of violent incidents or cases of harassment against the Jewish population.

Trafficking in Persons

See the Department of State's *Trafficking in Persons Report* at
www.state.gov/j/tip/rls/tiprpt/.

Persons with Disabilities

The law prohibits discrimination against persons with physical, sensory,
intellectual, and mental disabilities in employment, education, air travel and other
transport, access to health care, and provisions of state services, and it establishes
infractions and sanctions for noncompliance with specified norms. The law
provides for the protection, care, rehabilitation, security, and social inclusion of
persons with disabilities; mandates that public spaces be free of barriers and
accessible to persons with disabilities; and provides for the appointment of a
disability rights specialist in the Ombudsman's Office.

The law mandates that the government make its internet sites accessible for
persons with disabilities and requires the inclusion of sign language or subtitles in
all educational and cultural programs on public television and in media available in
all public libraries.

The government devoted limited resources to law enforcement and training on
disability issues, and many persons with disabilities remained economically and
socially marginalized. Governments at the national, regional, and local levels
made little effort to provide persons with disabilities with access to public
buildings. There were few interpreters for deaf persons in government offices and
no access to recordings or braille for blind persons. The majority of government
websites remained inaccessible to persons with disabilities, and only the
congressional television channel offered sign language interpretation. The
National Statistics and Information Institute (INEI) reported there were 18
registered sign language interpreters for more than 500,000 deaf persons. On
September 27, political parties represented in the 2016-2021 Congress created a
special caucus to work for the rights of persons with disabilities.

The government failed to enforce effectively laws protecting the rights of persons
with mental disabilities. NGOs reported the number of medical personnel
providing services in psychiatric institutions was insufficient to care for all
patients. The ombudsman and NGOs reported many children with disabilities
were unable to attend public schools due to lack of physical access.

While officials made advancements on the enforcement of the rights of persons
with disabilities during the year, the country's disability community still faced

immense challenges due to inaccessible infrastructure, minimal access to education, insufficient employment opportunities, and discrimination, according to a cross section of government and civil society leaders. During the year the Ombudsman's Office reported that approximately 87 percent of children with disabilities did not attend school and 76 percent of persons with disabilities did not work. One government survey reported that 70 percent of employers stated they would not hire a person with a disability.

National/Racial/Ethnic Minorities

The law requires the government to treat all citizens equally and forbids discrimination based on race, national origin, or language. Nevertheless, persons of indigenous and African descent (Afro-Peruvian) in particular faced societal discrimination and prejudice. Indigenous people and Afro-Peruvians remained underrepresented in leadership positions in government, business, and the military. Although the law prohibits mentioning race in job advertisements, employers often required applicants to submit photographs with their employment applications.

Racial discrimination, a small population size, lack of political representation, and a dispersed geographic location along the coast all contributed to the Afro-Peruvian community's political and economic underdevelopment. The Ministry of Culture reported in July that Afro-Peruvians had particular difficulties accessing health and education services. While the percentage of Afro-Peruvians ages 18 to 26 with access to higher education increased from 26 percent to 35 percent from 2004 to 2015, it remained below the national average of 43 percent. As of October, the 130-member Congress included two self-identified Afro-Peruvian representatives.

On July 15, the government adopted the National Plan for the Development of the Afro-Peruvian Population. The plan recognizes the rights of Afro-Peruvians and adopts principles and goals for improving the political, economic, and social development of the Afro-Peruvian community. Under the minister of culture's lead, a broad array of government ministries must adopt measures to gradually implement the National Plan and monitor its fulfillment.

Indigenous People

Indigenous communities remained politically, economically, and socially marginalized. The constitution and laws stipulate that all citizens have the right to use their own language before any authority through an interpreter. Quechua,

Aymara, and other indigenous languages share official status with Spanish in regions where citizens primarily speak these languages. Nevertheless, the government dedicated insufficient resources for interpretation services, impeding the full participation of indigenous persons in the political process.

Some indigenous persons living in remote areas lacked identity documents. In many cases the government did not have offices located in the areas where indigenous people lived. Additionally, NGOs and civil society leaders reported that some government officials allegedly sought bribes in exchange for documents, which indigenous persons were unable or unwilling to pay. Without identity cards, they were unable to exercise basic rights, such as voting and gaining access to health services and education.

While the constitution recognizes that indigenous persons have the right to own land communally, indigenous groups often lacked legal title to demarcate the boundaries of their lands, making it difficult to resist encroachment by outsiders. The granting of land titles remained slow. Amazonian indigenous people in particular accused the national government of delaying the final allocation of indigenous land titles. By law local communities retain the right of unassignability, which should prevent the reassignment of indigenous land titles to nonindigenous tenants. Some indigenous community members, however, sold land to outsiders without the majority consent of their community. The Ombudsman's Office reported the government took steps to assure government funds and other resources were available to improve Amazonian land-title policies.

Much of the conflict involving indigenous people in the Amazon related to extractive industry projects. By law the government holds the subsurface mineral rights for land throughout the country, which frequently caused disputes between the local indigenous communities, national government, regional government, and the various extractive interests. The law also requires the government to establish a database of indigenous communities entitled to consultation and produce a detailed implementation guide to facilitate government and private-sector compliance. Several indigenous organizations and the Ombudsman's Office expressed concern that indigenous communities did not have sufficient training to engage in consultations with the government and industry. As of January the government had concluded 18 agreements with indigenous communities and companies to undertake extractive projects.

Indigenous persons often faced threats from illegal miners and loggers who operated near or within their claimed land holdings. Indigenous leaders raised concerns that the government remained unable to protect indigenous communities from these threats, due in part to the relative isolation of indigenous communities within the Amazon provinces. As of December the 2014 killings of four Ashaninka indigenous leaders from the Alto Tamaya-Saweto community in the Amazon near the border with Brazil remained unsolved and under investigation.

Many indigenous persons and others with indigenous physical features faced societal discrimination and prejudice. They were often the victims of derogatory comments and illegal discrimination in public places, including theaters, restaurants, and clubs.

The Ministry of Culture created several tools to help protect the rights of indigenous people. These continued efforts included interpreter training, implementing guidelines for providing public services, and administrative processes for creating indigenous land reserves. The Ministry of Education operated bilingual schools in certain areas of the Amazon, maintaining special education programs in Spanish and the local indigenous language. As of October there were 30 institutes and nine universities offering training for teachers in bilingual education, with 1,790 teachers trained and 4,500 enrolled.

Acts of Violence, Discrimination, and Other Abuses Based on Sexual Orientation and Gender Identity

LGBTI persons remained some of the most marginalized individuals in the country and frequently were targets of discrimination. The law does not specifically prohibit discrimination against persons based on sexual orientation or gender identity, and the government did not keep national-level statistics on such discrimination. The government does not recognize same-sex marriage or civil unions. The constitutional procedure code, however, recognizes the right of individuals to file legal claims of discrimination based on sexual orientation or gender identity. Four of the regional governments (in Piura, La Libertad, Loreto, and San Martin) have regulations that prohibit discrimination against LGBTI individuals explicitly and provide for administrative relief but not criminal sanctions.

Government officials, NGOs, journalists, and civil society leaders reported official and societal discrimination against persons occurred based on their sexual orientation and gender identity in employment, housing, education, and health care. According to NGO and Ombudsman Office reports, government authorities, including the police, harassed and abused LGBTI persons, particularly transgender women. NGO studies revealed that law enforcement authorities repeatedly failed to protect, and on occasion violated, the rights of LGBTI citizens. Police violence and harassment particularly targeted transgender women, despite training.

The law does not provide transgender persons the right to identify with their gender or change their names on their national identity documents. The only path available to transgender people to change their names is through a long, unpredictable judicial process that frequently results in denial or at best enables them to adopt a "gender neutral" name. Transgender persons, therefore, often did not have national identification cards, which limited their access to government services.

Local NGOs reported that discrimination based on sexual orientation and gender identity was widespread, culturally sanctioned, and largely underreported due to fear of violence or additional discrimination. NGOs reported that LGBTI youth were frequently targets of severe bullying that contributed to higher rates of suicide than for non-LGBTI youth.

On August 31, the Ombudsman's Office became the first public institution to issue a report dedicated to LGBTI human rights.

Studies conducted by local NGOs indicated 95 percent of LGBTI citizens had experienced some type of violence or discrimination directed at them because of their status as LGBTI persons. On May 3, a 14-year-old transgender girl was shot and killed at a party after having been harassed for being transgender. While the alleged culprit faced criminal prosecution for the killing, he did not face hate crime charges.

On February 13, a group of LGBTI activists gathered in Lima's central square for an event called "Besos Contra Homofobia" (Kisses Against Homophobia). When the activists embraced and kissed, the police told them to leave the square. When the activists refused, police used a water cannon, shields, and clubs to push the activists out of the square. The government prohibits all protests in the central square, but since equally peaceful events have taken place there unbothered, LGBTI activists contended that PNP's response singled out LGBTI citizens and discriminated against their use of a public space.

HIV and AIDS Social Stigma

Persons with HIV/AIDS faced discrimination and harassment, including societal discrimination for employment, housing, and general social inclusion. The Ministry of Health implemented policies to combat discrimination based on HIV/AIDS status. HIV/AIDS affects transgender women disproportionately, and many of them could not obtain health care because they lacked national identification cards reflecting their gender and appearance.

Other Societal Violence or Discrimination

The Ombudsman's Office reported 154 active social conflict cases as of October. The report found that 71 percent of the social conflicts involved social-environmental issues, with mining-related incidents accounting for 63 percent of the cases. These conflicts disproportionately affected indigenous populations in the Andean and Amazon Regions. At times violence occurred during protests between the security forces and protesters.

Socio-environmental activist Maxima Acuna, who received the Goldman Environmental Prize in April, continued her long-running land dispute with a multinational mining corporation. Acuna and her family alleged the company had threatened and harassed them since 2011 in an effort to take their land. On September 18, Acuna and her husband clashed with the mining company's security guards, which resulted in moderate injuries to her and minor injuries to her husband. Officials were investigating the confrontation and reviewing Acuna's security. On September 28, a fact-finding report on the land dispute (financed by the company) faulted both parties for poor communication and the company for failing to assess the impact of its actions on Acuna. The report did not find conclusive evidence that the company committed human rights abuses.

The police shot and killed Quintino Cereceda during an October 14 protest against noise and pollution resulting from trucks transporting materials from the Las Bambas mine in a highland rural area of the Apurimac Region. Minister of Interior Carlos Basombrio declared the police operation was "unilateral and not consulted" with national authorities. Basombrio acknowledged the existence of problematic agreements between the mining company and local police that should be revised.

Section 7. Worker Rights

a. Freedom of Association and the Right to Collective Bargaining

With certain limitations, labor laws and regulations provide freedom of association, the right to strike, and collective bargaining. The law prohibits employer intimidation and other forms of antiunion discrimination and requires reinstatement of workers fired for union activity, unless they opt to receive compensation instead. Regulations allow workers to form unions without seeking prior authorization. The minimum membership required by law to form a union is 20 employees for a workplace-level union and 50 employees for a sector-wide union, which some labor activists viewed as prohibitively high in some instances, particularly for small and medium-sized enterprises.

The law specifies that public- and private-sector workers have the right to organize, bargain collectively, and strike, but it stipulates that the right to strike must be "in harmony with broader social objectives." The law prohibits judges, prosecutors, police officers, and military members from forming or joining unions. New unions must register in the Ministry of Labor and Employment Protection's Sub-directorate of Conflict Prevention under a process that takes up to four days, during which time employers may dismiss unionized workers and leaders.

The law allows unions to declare a strike in accordance with their governing documents. Private- and public-sector union workers must give advance notice of a strike to the employer and the Ministry of Labor. Private-sector workers must give advance notice of at least five working days, and public-sector workers must give at least 10 days' notice. The law also allows nonunion workers to declare a strike with a majority vote as long as the written voting record is notarized and announced at least five working days prior to a strike. Unions in essential services are permitted to call a strike but must provide 15 working days' notice, receive the approval of the ministry, be approved by a simple majority of workers, and provide a sufficient number of workers during a strike to maintain operations. Private enterprises and the public institutions cannot fire workers who strike legally. The private sector, however, can fire illegally striking workers on the fourth day of their unapproved absence. The public sector can fire illegal striking employees sector through an administrative procedure.

Unless there is a pre-existing labor contract covering an occupation or industry as a whole, unions must negotiate with companies individually. The law establishes processes for direct negotiations and conciliation. If these mechanisms fail, workers may declare a strike or request arbitration. The law outlines the process that authorizes the use of arbitration to end collective labor disputes. The law gives a party the ability to compel the other party to submit to arbitration (whether worker- or employer-initiated) whenever either of the parties cannot reach an agreement in the first collective bargaining negotiation, or a party does not engage in good faith during collective bargaining by delaying, hindering, or avoiding an agreement. If the parties disagree over whether or not a prerequisite for binding arbitration was met, the law also allows a party to submit the matter to independent, nongovernmental arbitrators for an initial decision.

The law requires businesses to monitor their contractors with respect to labor rights, and imposes liability on businesses for the actions of their contractors. The law governing the general private-sector labor regime sets out nine different categories of short-term employment contracts that companies may use to hire workers based on particular circumstances. The law sets time limits for each of the categories and contains a five-year overall limit on the consecutive use of short-term employment contracts when contracts from different categories are used together. A sector-specific law covering the nontraditional export sectors (e.g., fishing, wood and paper, nonmetallic minerals, jewelry, textiles and apparel, and the agriculture industry) exempts employers from this five-year limit and allows employers in those sectors to hire workers on a series of short-term contracts indefinitely, without requiring a conversion to the permanent workforce.

The government did not effectively enforce freedom of association and collective bargaining laws. Resources remained inadequate, including for the Ministry of Labor and its National Superintendency of Labor Inspection (SUNAFIL). Penalties for violations of freedom of association and collective bargaining range from 7,400 to 74,000 soles ($2,240 to $22,400). Such penalties were insufficient to deter violations and, according to labor experts and union representatives, were rarely enforced. Workers faced prolonged judicial processes and lack of enforcement following dismissals resulting from trade union activity. For example, NGOs reported that emblematic cases of labor arbitration dating from 2012 remained suspended, with the implementation of arbitrators' decisions delayed by judicial appeals processes. NGOs also reported instances of noncompliance with arbitrators' decisions.

Workers faced challenges in exercising their freedom of association and collective bargaining rights. Unions and labor experts reported that the labor ministry refused to register newly affiliated union members after the initial union registration period concluded. Employers continued to dismiss workers for exercising their right to strike. Dismissals of striking workers and delays in reinstatement of these workers, in both legal and illegal strikes, were the main tactic used by employers to dissuade workers from going on strike. This was particularly acute at the Marsa and Shougang mines, which had majority-subcontracted workforces.

Labor union representatives and labor sector experts continued to report cases of employers who filed criminal charges against workers who engaged in strikes. These charges, which alleged material damage, then served as the basis for dismissing union officers and workers who participated in strikes. Union members also expressed concern that some employers were using criminal investigations as an intimidation tactic prior to impending collective bargaining activities. During the year an agricultural export company allegedly tried to intimidate the Solidarity Center labor organization Lima office by threatening legal action against its leadership. The company threatened to file a defamation lawsuit over letters the organization had sent the company's buyers, which claimed the company's actions undermined union leadership. The company, however, did not follow through with its threatened lawsuit.

Significant delays in the collective bargaining process were a common obstacle to compliance with worker rights to bargain collectively. In many cases employers showed a lack of interest in concluding agreements. Workers employed under laws to promote the textile, apparel, and agriculture industries faced obstacles, such as allegations of delayed negotiations and legal threats, to exercise the right to collective bargaining.

An antiunion practice some employers used during the rating period included using subcontracting to avoid direct employment relationships. Such subcontracting also limited the size of a company's permanent workforce, making it more difficult to reach the 20-employee threshold necessary to form a union.

Many businesses, including export industries, hired temporary workers, who were effectively unable to join unions because they feared their contracts might not be renewed. Employers also circumvented restrictions regarding hiring temporary workers to perform core company functions. Unions, NGOs, and some multinational apparel brands criticized the law on nontraditional export sectors and its exemption from limits on the consecutive use of short-term employment contracts, asserting that workers employed under it and who attempted to organize or affiliate with unions did not have their contracts renewed.

Labor unions, however, also reported positive developments. In one case union representatives and management officials with a large agricultural company agreed to convert 3,000 short-term workers to permanent positions. The unions acknowledged that the seasonal nature of this company's particular agricultural activity made it difficult for the company to convert its entire workforce to permanent positions. As a result the union and agricultural company reached an agreement to give 5,000 short-term workers, who did not receive permanent positions, hiring preferences during the growing season.

NGOs reported management interference in labor-management health and safety committees. Management sometimes interfered in the election of worker representatives, held committee sessions without full worker representation, and failed to notify elected worker representatives when labor inspectors conducted workplace inspections.

b. Prohibition of Forced or Compulsory Labor

The law prohibits all forms of forced or compulsory labor, but the government did not effectively enforce the law.

Resources, inspections, and remediation were inadequate for effective enforcement of the law. The law prescribes penalties of eight to 25 years' imprisonment for labor trafficking, although the government did not report statistics on convictions and sentences for forced labor during the year. Financial penalties for violations range from 7,400 to 74,000 soles ($2,240 to $22,400) but were insufficient to deter violations.

SUNAFIL officials conducted inspections to identify forced labor. The Ministry of Labor and SUNAFIL provided training sessions to SUNAFIL and regional labor inspectors around the country to raise awareness of forced labor and the applicable law. The government also implemented the 2013-2017 national plan to combat forced labor. Sector experts repeated their criticisms of the plan for not containing a dedicated national budget, which made implementation difficult.

Thousands of persons remained subject to conditions of forced labor, mainly in mining, forestry, agriculture, brick making, and domestic service. There were reports that men and boys were subjected to bonded labor in mining (including gold mining), forestry, and brick making, while women were most often found working under conditions of domestic servitude. Both men and women were reported working in bonded labor in agriculture.

On April 15, the PNP rescued 114 victims of labor and sex trafficking during a large raid on 15 makeshift bar-brothels located just outside the Tambopata Natural

Reserve in the Madre de Dios region of Peru. The 114 rescued adult victims included 113 women, one of whom was nine months pregnant. All the victims were Peruvian nationals from various remote towns and small villages throughout the country. The police detained 28 alleged human traffickers, also all Peruvian, who are in jail awaiting prosecution.

Also see the Department of State's *Trafficking in Persons Report* at www.state.gov/j/tip/rls/tiprpt/.

c. Prohibition of Child Labor and Minimum Age for Employment

The legal minimum age for employment is 14, although children between ages 12 and 14 may work in certain jobs for up to four hours per day. Adolescents between ages 15 and 17 may work up to six hours per day, if they obtain special permission from the Ministry of Labor and certify that they are attending school. In certain sectors of the economy, higher age minimums existed: 15 in nonindustrial agriculture; 16 in industry, commerce, and mining; and 17 in industrial fishing. The law specifically prohibits the hiring of minors in a number of occupations considered hazardous for children, including working underground, lifting or carrying heavy weights, accepting responsibility for the safety of others, and working at night. The law prohibits work that jeopardizes the health of children and adolescents; puts their physical, mental, and emotional development at risk; or prevents regular attendance at school.

A permit from the labor ministry is required for persons under 18 to work legally. Parents must apply for the permits, and employers must have a permit on file to hire a youth.

The Ministry of Labor and SUNAFIL are responsible for enforcing child labor laws, but enforcement was not effective. The ministry and SUNAFIL lacked the resources needed to execute necessary inspections, and interministerial coordination was often lacking. Officials reported that inspectors conducted routine visits without notice to areas where persons or organizations reported child labor problems. By law the penalties for illegal child labor include fines from 192,500 new soles ($58,300) for microbusiness to 385,000 new soles ($117,000) for small and medium-sized businesses and 770,000 new soles ($233,000) for larger enterprises. In addition to these fines, violators are subject to civil and criminal legal proceedings.

The labor ministry continued the "Vamos Peru" (Let's Go, Peru) program, focused on job training, technical assistance to entrepreneurs, and job placement, and the "Peru Responsable" (Responsible Peru) program, aimed at fostering corporate social responsibility and creating formal employment for youth. The ministry continued to implement its national strategy to combat child labor, including projects in Junin, Huancavelica, Pasco, Carabayllo, and Huanuco, which focused on reducing child labor by improving educational services, providing mechanical tools, and providing cash transfers to families in rural areas.

The Office of the Ombudsman for Children and Adolescents (DEMUNA) worked with the labor ministry to document complaints regarding violations of child labor laws. DEMUNA operated a decentralized child labor reporting and tracking system. The Ministry of Women and Vulnerable Populations administered a program that sent specialized teachers to the streets to provide education and support to minors involved in begging and other kinds of work. The ministry continued to implement the Yachay program, which assists street children ages six to 17 with workshops, health care, education, legal services, and scholarships.

Child labor remained a serious problem, especially in the informal sector. In 2014 INEI estimated there were 1.65 million children working in exploitative labor conditions. The worst forms of child labor generally occurred in the informal sectors, including in commercial sexual exploitation (see section 6, Children), gold mining, brick and fireworks manufacturing, stone extraction, forestry, and agriculture, including the production of Brazil nuts and coca. In many cases children worked alongside their parents in a family business, usually in areas and sectors cited above.

Representatives from the labor ministry, NGOs, and labor unions reported counterfeit U.S. currency cases that involved child labor. Police rescued minors while engaged in operations against U.S. currency counterfeiters. The labor ministry, NGOs, and labor activists reported the use of child labor in rice production on plantations in the Tumbes Region.

Also, see the Department of Labor's *Findings on the Worst Forms of Child Labor* at www.dol.gov/ilab/reports/child-labor/findings/.

d. Discrimination with Respect to Employment and Occupation

The law prohibits discrimination with respect to employment based on race, color, sex, religion, political opinion, national origin, citizenship, social origin, disability, age, language, or social status. The law does not specifically identify discrimination based on sexual orientation and/or gender identity, HIV-positive status, or other communicable diseases. The law prohibits discrimination against domestic workers and any requirement by employers for their domestic workers to wear uniforms in public places. The law establishes the following employment quotas for persons with disabilities: 3 percent for private businesses with more than 50 employees and 5 percent for public-sector organizations. The National Council for the Integration of Persons with Disabilities oversees compliance with employment quotas for persons with disabilities.

The government did not effectively enforce the law. Penalties for violations included fines and imprisonment, but they were not sufficient to deter violations. NGOs and labor rights advocates noted that discrimination cases often went unreported to authorities, in part due to a lack of confidence in the legal system to address the case.

Numerous violations of provisions prohibiting discrimination against domestic workers and any requirement by employers for their domestic workers to wear uniforms in public places were reported during the year. The Ministry of Labor, local NGOs, and several unions continued campaigns to inform domestic workers about their rights.

Societal prejudice and discrimination also led to disproportionate poverty and unemployment rates for women. Women were more likely to work in the informal sector or in less secure occupations, such as domestic service, factory workers, or street vendors, and they were more likely to be illiterate due to lack of formal education.

e. Acceptable Conditions of Work

The statutory monthly minimum wage for formal workers was 850 soles ($251). INEI estimated the poverty line to be 315 soles ($93) a month per person, although it varied by region. As of September the average monthly income rose 6 percent, compared with the previous year--1,640 soles ($487) to 1,867 soles ($495) for men and 1,352 ($401) for women.

The law provides for a 48-hour workweek for formal workers and one day of rest, and it requires premium pay for overtime. There is no prohibition on excessive compulsory overtime, nor does the law limit the amount of overtime that a worker may work. The law stipulates certain rights and benefits to which adult domestic workers are entitled, such as an eight-hour workday, no work on public holidays, 15 days of paid annual vacation, and salary bonuses in July and December. The law grants administrative service contract workers who meet minimum service requirements 30 days of vacation, June and December bonuses, and up to three months of severance pay in the case of unjustified dismissal.

The government sets occupational health and safety standards appropriate for the main industries in the country, but sector experts reported that government resources and expertise were not sufficient to maintain appropriate health and safety standards. The law allows workers to remove themselves from situations that endanger health or safety without jeopardy to their employment. The law also enables employers to outsource the management of health and safety to third-party service providers and restrict democratically elected worker representatives from obtaining leave to attend to their safety and health duties, including training.

The government often did not devote sufficient personnel, technical, and financial resources to enforce occupational safety and health regulations and other labor laws. As of October SUNAFIL, the government body charged with labor inspection duties, reported having 394 inspectors nationwide, 167 in Lima and the rest assigned to Arequipa, Tumbes, La Libertad, Cajamarca, Loreto, Ancash, Huanuco, Ica, and Moquegua Regions. The labor ministry and regional governments had an additional 88 labor inspectors.

Fines for labor violations were last increased in April 2014. Noncompliance with the law is punishable by fines of 7,400 to 74,000 soles ($2,240 to $22,400). In July 2014, however, the government enacted a three-year decree that reduced fines on employers for labor violations to no more than 35 percent of the maximum fine established by law. The reduction appeared limited to reducing fines for occupational safety and health violations that do not result in death or permanent injury of the worker and violations of laws related to freedom of association and workplace discrimination that are determined not to be "very serious." The reduction did not apply to violations that "very seriously affect" freedom of association, union formation, and workplace discrimination; violations related to child labor or forced labor; violations of occupational and safety norms that result in death or permanent disability of the worker; actions that impede labor inspections; and recidivist conduct, defined as repeat violations within a six-month period from the time a final decision on the first infraction was issued. Penalties were insufficient to deter violations. Many fines went uncollected, in part because the government lacked an efficient tracking system and at times due to a lack of political will, according to a local labor NGO.

The law provides for fines and criminal sanctions for occupational safety and health violations. In cases of infractions, injury, or deaths of workers or subcontractors, the penalty is one to four years' imprisonment. Criminal penalties are limited to those cases where employers have "deliberately" violated safety and health laws and where labor authorities have previously notified employers who have chosen not to adopt measures in response to a repeated infraction. The law requires that a worker prove an employer's culpability to obtain compensation for work-related injuries.

Labor, businesses, and the government reported that the majority of companies in the formal sector generally complied with the law. Many workers in the informal economy, approximately 70 percent of the total labor force, received less than the minimum wage, although most were self-employed. Employers often interfered with the formation and operation of labor-management committees by influencing elections for labor representatives and limiting committee power.

Employers frequently required long hours from domestic workers and paid low wages. NGOs and union officials continued to report allegations of abuse of subcontracted workers in the areas of wage and hour violations, and associational rights. In 2015 a group of 34 outsourced workers at the Aceros Arequipa steel plant in Pisco, who had previously filed a labor inspection complaint, were told their contracts were not compliant, and they were all dismissed. As of November the union was seeking their reinstatement.

Union members and labor-sector experts reported that regional and national statistical registers did not reflect the number of severe and fatal injuries from workplace accidents that occurred in the mining, electrical, and construction sectors. Workplace labor, health, and safety committees continued to develop across the country. Labor experts and NGOs expressed concern about what they considered an unreasonably high threshold for holding employers accountable for workplace injuries and for not maintaining health and safety standards.